HOW TO OVERCOME LONELINESS

Metropolitan Youssef

ST MARY & MOSES ABBEY PRESS

How to Overcome Loneliness
By Metropolitan Youssef

Designed & Published by:
St. Mary & St. Moses Abbey Press
101 S Vista Dr, Sandia, TX 78383
stmabbeypress.com

Translation from Arabic by St. Mary & St. Moses Abbey.

Contents

CHAPTER 1

Introduction

Sometimes a person feels empty and detached, that is, detached from others, and he is haunted by the feeling that he is unimportant and worthless, that he is undesirable, that those among whom he lives do not love him. This is the feeling of loneliness.

This person does not usually have close friendships with others. The feeling of loneliness is also related to a person's view of himself. A person who feels unloved has low self-esteem, even though he may be truly loved by people, yet he is the one who feels in himself that he is unloved and undesirable. Genetic factors may also play a role in a person's feeling of loneliness, for some scientists have discovered that there are specific genes controlling this. And there are also some mental illnesses, such as social anxiety, that make a person incapable of dealing with others, and then he becomes detached from them, and the feeling of loneliness develops in him. In addition to this, the cause may also be attributed to some biological illnesses. And the feeling of loneliness is different from solitude or retreat.

1

Loneliness and Solitude

There is a difference between solitude or taking a retreat and loneliness, and we will explain the difference between them as follows:

1. Solitude is that a person takes the decision by himself to live alone, by his own will, whether because of some personal circumstances, or by his own choice, as is the case in monasticism. As St. Isaac says, "Solitude in monasticism is the separation[1] from all, to unite with the One." As for loneliness, it is not a voluntary decision.

2. Solitude is a positive thing because it is under the control of man, for he is the one choosing it, desiring it, and then deciding [to do] it. As for loneliness, it is not under the control of man.

Therefore, we say that monks live the life of solitude and not the life of loneliness, for they went

1   Literally: dissolution.

into solitude entirely by their own will.

3. The feeling of loneliness does not require that a person be far from people, for a person might be living with others, and he nevertheless feels lonely. And a person may be surrounded by many people, yet his feeling of loneliness increases. For the feeling of loneliness springs from within.

And someone may seek marriage because he is alone and feels lonely, and may attribute this to being unmarried, but this is not true. So he decides to get married, yet he, nevertheless, feels lonely. Therefore, such a person should first overcome this feeling, before embarking on getting married, so that this will not be the basis of marital problems later.

2

The Definition of Loneliness

Loneliness is a feeling of detachment from people, even if the person were amidst a crowd, there being a big gap between him and others. The person sometimes feels that no one understands him or sympathizes with him, and no one connects with him.

Loneliness is an unsatisfied desire for love and connection with others, and this person finds it difficult to satisfy it. Perhaps the real reason for the inability of this person to connect with others is the lack of love within him, for if he sowed love, he would reap love too. This is a kind of selfishness, for he wants people to love him while he does not have the readiness to offer this love. He wants others to connect with him though he does not have the readiness himself to connect with them.

The feeling of loneliness may be accompanied by

a feeling of low self-esteem and of being worthless and unimportant, and this may consequently lead a person to despair, as a result of the constant [inner] feeling of rejection. We should however realize that all these feelings are only within this person and do not reflect the true reality outside of him.

The person who feels lonely is like a person who has lost someone very much dear to him, so this person feels the loss, which is the same feeling a lonely person has.

And the difference between the feeling of being alone—or the desire for independence—and the feeling of loneliness is that the former is a normal, healthy, and beneficial matter, but loneliness is an illness.

The person, at the time of their birth, experiences the feeling of separation, for the baby who was in their mother's womb for nine months, is separated from their mother when they were born. But the human soul of a person grows through connecting [i.e. forming attachments] with others and separating from others, so they grow in the way of independence and maturity, so that when they have reached the age of maturity, they would have a balance between his attachment to others and their remaining independent from them. And this is the state we call interdependence, that is, how he deals with others; he depends on them, and they depend on him, but he keeps his boundaries.

Therefore, it happens sometimes, when a person stays away from others with his own will and decides to separate from them for a particular period [of time], that this would enrich his life and help him to become mature. For if the infant remains attached to his father and mother his whole life, [he will have negative issues]; therefore, detachment must take place, that he may become disciplined, and his life may become healthy.

And it happens sometimes that the fathers and mothers delay the onset of detachment in the life of their children, and by this they impede their growth and maturity.

Loneliness is a sweeping feeling of isolation, despite that the person may be in the midst of a crowd. But gloominess[2] may be generated in the heart, making them depressed and sad, and the feeling of abandonment arises in him, so he feels that all [people] have abandoned him, and this makes him feel insecure too. And then he may reach despair and loss of the meaning of life, all these making him turn into a rebellious person against society, and [making him] violent.

If the feeling of loneliness increased within a person, and he became fully convinced that he is unloved and undesirable, then he would distance himself fully from others and would avoid them. This however will make him lonelier, and then he

---

2   Or: depression.

will go into a vicious cycle.

Of the curious matters, concerning loneliness, which were observed, is that they found that the lonely person turns creative and inventive. For there are people who feel lonely, yet they have composed wonderful musical pieces, and there are others who have painted the most beautiful paintings. Nevertheless, this does not make us conclude that loneliness creates innovativeness nor inventiveness in man's life. But what happens is that if a man were already talented in a particular field, like painting, music, poetry, or writing, then loneliness makes them excel all the more in their talent. This loneliness may polish these talents, thereby making the talented person produce a creative and inventive product.

3

The Causes of Loneliness

1. Research has shown that loneliness may begin from childhood. If a young child was brought up without being taught how to form friendships in his life, then when he reaches adolescence, having no friendships in life, it would be difficult for him to form friendships afterwards. Therefore, the feeling of loneliness would continue with him. The child may have formed friendships, but not with people who had a positive impact on his life, and therefore he will feel lonely when he grows up. This makes clear the importance of the role of fathers and mothers in encouraging their children to form valuable and meaningful friendships in their childhood. And this does not mean, for example, that other children may hit the child and take advantage of him, and yet he continues to be their friend and plays with them. But by positive impact, it is meant that other children respect him, love him, and appreciate him.

2. The cause may be organic diseases, whereby a person may be suffering of a chronic depression which has continued with him for a long time, and because of this depression, he distances himself from people and loses his friendships. And [consequently], this makes him feel lonely.

3. One of the very important causes of loneliness is that the child was left alone in infancy, as it happens in the cases of divorce. The father and mother may dispute with one another over who would get custody of the child. And it may happen that neither of them wants to take the child with them, and then the child feels abandoned, especially [coming] from people who do impact his life.

Divorce causes loneliness for the following three reasons:

Divorce is the loss of a permanent relationship with one of the parents or both, or the loss of a permanent relationship with the other [spouse] with respect to the husband or wife. The person was within a family, in a stable relationship, as is the case with respect to the child in his relationship with the father and mother, but after the divorce took place, the child found himself far away from the father or mother, and consequently lost this relationship. The same also happens with the husband and wife when they separate from each other. Both of them feel unwanted and unloved, because the other spouse left them.

Some say that divorce may sometimes be more harrowing upon the person than the death of the spouse. The reason for this is that the spouse who is still alive knows that the other spouse who died used to love them. As for the case of divorce, the other spouse has decided to leave them because of hatred, and that the spouse cannot bear to live with them.

Divorce makes a person feels lonely because of the climate that accompanies the divorce, and the sorrow, problems, and fights resulting from it.

The members of the family, in which a divorce has taken place, usually stay away from the social circles surrounding them, because they cannot appear together as a family. For example, when they receive an invitation to a party or for dinner, if the husband goes to this party, the wife will not go, and vice versa. And they do not go to church, so as to avoid being embarrassed by how people look at them.

4. Loneliness may occur because of changes that take place in life. For example, when someone gets married, they may feel lonely because of the transition from living in a family to living with another person, especially if this person was not accustomed to staying away from their family. Or there may be someone who has migrated from one country to another, or who has moved from one job to another, etc.

5. Even in the field of relationships, a person may feel lonely. For example, if there were a friendship between a person and another—or even within the frame of marriage—problems and disagreements may occur between them. When one of them becomes extremely angry, hatred arising in him, this person finds themself incapable of offering or receiving love, and consequently the feeling of loneliness grows more and more in the person.

6. Another cause for loneliness is that a person may lack communication skills. For example, a person may be shy and may not know how to communicate with others. Or the person may not know how to take the initiative.

Therefore, a person must learn how to adapt to changes and to develop their communication skills, in order to overcome loneliness.

4

Types of Loneliness and Their Symptoms

We will look into three types of loneliness and their symptoms.

1. The circumstantial or spatial type: That is, loneliness which is related to a circumstance or place; for example, someone migrating from one country to another, this is related to place. Or someone who lost a close friend, this is related to circumstance.

2. The developmental type: For example, a young child who is very attached to his parents, and a balance did not take place between attachment and independence. Therefore, the child would feel lonely when he grows up.

3. The internal type: It is the feeling of inadequacy, weakness, or rejection by others. And there may be more than one type at the same the

time.

As for the symptoms of loneliness, they are the following:

1. The person who feels lonely often feels that there is something wrong and there is no one who could understand them or appreciate their circumstances. And then the person feels that they have difficulty communicating with anyone.

2. This person gradually loses trust in themself, for they have doubts whether others love them, and then they hesitate considerably before doing anything, for fear that if they did something, it might be rejected. Therefore, they feel depressed and are afraid of speaking to anyone or taking the initiative, so that they may not encounter rejection. And consequently, this rejection leads to loneliness. And while they are avoiding this matter, they sink deeper into the mire of loneliness.

3. This person is also suffering from a vast internal void. For they may be very busy, yet they are suffering from a void and dissatisfaction within themself, and perhaps this may lead them to clinical depression.

5

The Effect of Modern Society on Loneliness

Unfortunately, the feeling of loneliness is very much increasing in modern society. Research has shown that loneliness is much greater in crowded cities and communities than in small cities and rural communities. This has also been observed in church service. For there may be a region consisting of twenty or thirty families, and there are large churches in which the number of families may reach to about five hundred. It was found that people who live in small regions know each other and deal with each other, and this makes them communicate well with one another.

Frequent dealings in such small communities provide an opportunity to form new relationships that help a person overcome loneliness, and the person feels that this small church is as though one family.

But if a person moves from this small community to a large church which has a large congregation, you will find that he does not know anyone, and it is difficult for him to deal with people. And every time he goes to church, he finds new people beside him, or he may talk to a few people, yet no one feels for the other, and therefore he feels that he is lonely in the midst of this large community.

Statistics have been taken in this field, showing that at the beginning of the twentieth century, in the year 1900, only 5% of the population of the United States of America were suffering from loneliness, but at the end of the twentieth century, in 1998, it was found that 25% of the population of the United States were suffering from loneliness. In 1995, there were 24 million people in the United States living with loneliness, and the number rose to 31 million in 2010, and this explains the impact of modern societies on man's feeling of loneliness. This feeling represents the most common complaint among people.

In 1985, it was found that the average American citizen had three friends, meaning that each citizen had three close friends, and in 2006, this number went down to two. In 1985, people who had no friends at all constituted 10% of the population, and in 2006, the percentage rose to 25%. It was also found that the number of people who have one friend in their lives, and this friend is most probably a very close person to them like a husband or wife, has reached 19% in 2006.

The reasons leading to this may be attributed to the following:

1. Excessive busyness that does not permit people to have the time to communicate with each other. In Egyptian society, for example, work used to end at around two in the afternoon, then the employee would return to their home and rest for a while after lunch. And in the afternoon, there is [enough] time to get to know each other, to visit one another, to form relationships, and to do spiritual services.

As for now, you may find a person working in the morning and then working again in the evening, in order to increase his income. And the wife also works, and then there is no time for relationships.

2. Technology. Technology has led to a lack of face-to-face communications between people. The husband may be sitting in one room and the wife in another, and yet he sends her text messages. There are no direct relationships; rather e-mails and Facebook have replaced them. Technology has destroyed many of the human relationships. And when television was discovered, it was said that it would be a means of bonding between family members while they watched TV shows, and there would be room for talking with each other, but what happened is that every person likes to watch a different show from that which the other person likes to watch. And there may be more than one television in the same home, which contributed to turning the home into a hotel, where each person occupies a room of his own, and this has contributed to the disintegration of the family.

3. Materialism. The person currently pants for material things. Therefore, he works more in order to greatly increase the amount of money he has, and sacrifices relationships in order to increase his balance in the bank. And for this reason, he moves from one city to another, in search of more material things. This makes him feel lonelier.

4. Selfishness. The world nowadays feeds and fuels selfishness and self-centeredness. The husband no longer sacrifices for the sake of the family and others, nor puts others' interests before his own. For example, this is what happens in the case of divorce. For the husband seeks divorce because he does not feel happy, and the interest of the children is of no interest to him.

> *"There is nothing under heaven that perturbs nor upsets me, because I am sheltered under that impregnable fort, within that trusted refuge, reassured in the bosom of mercies, possessing a fountain of consolation."*
>
> — H.H. Pope St. Kyrillos VI —

6

The Danger of Loneliness

1. All of us, without exception, have gone through one period or another in our life wherein we felt lonely. This is normal and there is no fault in it. There are many people in the Holy Scriptures who have experienced this feeling, and I can even dare to say that the Lord Jesus Christ Himself experienced this feeling when He said, "And [all of you] will leave me alone." But the feeling of loneliness may become chronic, that is, accompanying the person continually, so the person suffers from what is called clinical depression. This is more dangerous than the feeling of fear and anxiety, because if I am afraid or anxious, I can look for someone to help me. But in the case of depression, a person feels lonely and that there is no one in his life who can lend him a hand. And in the book of Ecclesiastes, he says, "Woe to him who is alone when he falls, for he has no one to

help him up."[3] That is, a person who is lonely will not find anyone to help him up if he falls, having no one in his mind. And this is what happened with the man who was at the pool of Bethesda and was sick for thirty-eight years. He said to the Lord Christ, "I have no man to put me into the pool."[4] This is the feeling of loneliness.

2. Sometimes there may be a person who has one friend, so he multiplies his requests of this friend and becomes very demanding of him, and constantly asks him, "Why do you no longer love me? Why don't you spend time with me? Why do you leave me?" The friend may feel suffocated by the many requests, so he distances himself from him, and then he loses the only friend he had. This further fuels his loneliness, and he feels all the more the bitterness of loneliness, along with feeling increasingly troubled and distressed.

3. Some research studies have shown that there is a relationship between chronic loneliness and some diseases like cancer, heart diseases, insomnia, and in some cases, it might lead to suicide.

4. Loneliness may end up leading to addiction, so this person would become addicted to alcohol or some drug or medication.

5. The feeling of loneliness may also lead to extravagance. This person who is feeling lonely

---

3   Ecclesiastes 4:10.

4   John 5: 7.

would then want to spoil themself by buying many things, thinking that these things would make them happy, but in the end, they discover that none of them makes them happy.

6. Loneliness may also lead to some moral deviations, so a person practices sin with anyone, in pursuit of filling the void which he feels. Therefore, he makes sinful relationships. Loneliness may lead children to become violent, and it may lead to a delay in growth and education.

It is found that the most susceptible people to loneliness are youth and middle-aged individuals who have not been married, and the elderly.

7

Biblical Examples

There are fathers and saints in the Holy Scriptures who suffered from loneliness, such as David, who says in Psalm 142, "Look on my right hand and see, for there is no one who acknowledges me; refuge has failed me; no one cares for my soul."[5] And in Psalm 102, he says:

> For my days are consumed like smoke,—[he likens life to smoke, a vapor that appears for a little time and then vanishes away[6]]— and my bones are burned like a hearth [that is, there is no joy but sorrow of heart]. My heart is stricken and withered like grass, so that I forget to eat my bread. Because of the sound of my groaning my bones cling to my skin [that is, I have become skin and

5   Psalms 142:4.
6   See James 4:14.

bone]. I am like a pelican of the wilderness [which has no friends]; I am like an owl of the desert [which has no friends either]. I lie awake, and am like a sparrow alone on the housetop. My enemies reproach me all day long; those who deride me swear an oath against me. [That is, all men are against men and hate me]. For I have eaten ashes like bread, and mingled my drink with weeping.[7]

All these verses strongly express David's feeling of loneliness. This took place perhaps when he was fleeing from Saul. This made him feel that all people were against him. Nevertheless, David eliminated loneliness with the same treatment which psychology presents to us [today] and which we will discuss in the next chapter.

---

7   Psalms 102:3–9

8

The Treatment for Loneliness

We will first discuss the methods of treatment presented by psychology, and then we will talk about the treatment provided by the Holy Scriptures. We will see that the basis of treatment in psychology is found in the Holy Scriptures, for it has not provided anything new.

1. The treatment of loneliness depends on studying its causes. For a person should examine the reason for this feeling within him, and then should reverse the negative thoughts, feelings, and inclinations which he has. For example, if a person is convinced that no one loves him, we can make clear to him that there are people in his life who do love him, and that he should be renewed in his mind and look at matters with a realistic and sound view, as the Apostle Paul says, "Be transformed by

the renewing of your mind."[8]

2. It was also found that group therapy is very useful in this case. When a person is in the middle of a group, this creates an opportunity for him to communicate, and will help him form relationships, and then he can overcome loneliness.

3. Some psychiatrists use some medications and antidepressants. However, the majority of them do not resort to these medications and prefer the use sports, proper nutrition, and acceptable means of entertainment.

4. One of the treatment methods is the retrieval of beautiful memories of the past. For example, an elderly person may be taken to the place where he was brought up as a child, especially if this place had left beautiful memories for him. Bringing back beautiful memories can greatly help with the treatment. This is the reason for the sake of which the Lord commanded us to celebrate feasts. And the word "feast" in Arabic is derived from the word "bringing back," meaning "to bring back a beautiful memory" or "to commemorate this memory."

5. Let us remember that the Lord Christ, to Him be the glory, passed through these feelings, for He took three disciples with Him, and when they slept and left Him, He admonished them, saying, "What! Could you not watch with Me one hour?"[9] And it

8   Romans 12:2.
9   Matthew 26:40.

was said concerning Him when He was on the cross, "And from the people no one was with Me."[10] And He said to the disciples, "And [you] will leave Me alone. And yet I am not alone."[11] Our Lord Jesus Christ passed through these feelings; therefore, our teacher Paul says, "For in that He Himself has suffered, being tempted, He is able to aid those who are tempted."[12]

Therefore, a person who feels lonely, if he enters into the presence of God and begins to pray, to pour out his soul, and to seek comfort from Him, he will say with David the prophet, "When my father and my mother forsake me, then the LORD will take care of me."[13] And he also says in the psalm, "I cried out to You, O LORD: I said, 'You are my refuge, my portion in the land of the living. Attend to my cry, for I am brought very low; deliver me from my persecutors, for they are stronger than I. Bring my soul out of prison, that I may praise Your name; the righteous shall surround me, for You shall deal bountifully with me.'"[14] The person who feels lonely feels exactly as though he is in prison, and if a severe punishment befalls the accused, he is placed in solitary confinement; that is, he is completely isolated from the rest. The feeling of loneliness is

---

10   Isaiah 63:3.

11   John 16:32.

12   Hebrews 2:18.

13   Psalms 27:10.

14   Psalms 142:5–7.

the confinement in which a person places himself.

6. Take to yourself the Lord as a friend, a father, and a shepherd, as David the prophet said, "When my father and my mother forsake me, then the LORD will take care of me."[15] It says in Hebrews, "For He Himself said, 'I will not leave you nor forsake you.' So we may boldly say: 'The Lord is my helper; I will not fear. What can man do to me?'"[16] And in the psalm, he says, "Yea, though I walk through the valley of the shadow of death, I will fear no evil; for You are with me."[17]

7. Of the things that help a person come out of loneliness is to examine his gifts and to use them to serve others and those in need, as the Holy Scripture says, "As each one has received a gift, minister it to one another, as good stewards of the manifold grace of God."[18] In the service, there is communication with others, and a loving relationship will be formed between the one serving and those served, and the servant's heart will be opened through love, so those served will feel that they are loved and desired.

8. Also surround yourself with spiritual friends. Form friendships for yourself. And if you have one friend, do not exhaust him, nor make him feel weary of you, as the Bible says, "Seldom set foot in your neighbor's house, lest he become weary of you and

---

15 Psalms 27:10.
16 Hebrews 13:5–6.
17 Psalms 23:4.
18 1 Peter 4:10.

hate you."[19] Be kind and loving, and others will love you, and then, you can form friendships.

> *"If you have God, then you have everything, even though you are deprived of everything. And if you do not have God, then you are deprived of everything, even though you possess everything."*
>
> — Saint Anthony —

9. In your many preoccupations, focus on relationships and the human aspect. That I finish a project I am working on is not the only important thing, such that all my attention is concentrated on it, but the people I deal with are important too. And do not give in to destructive thoughts which make you think that people reject you, but say with Paul the Apostle: "I can do all things through Christ who strengthens me."[20]

10. Participate in group activities as much as you can, whether on trips or through group services.

In conclusion, a mature Christian must have a balance between a life of solitude and a successful social life. He must spend time with God in solitude, as Mary the sister of Lazarus did, that he may be filled with the love of God, and must also practice social relationships with others.

---

19   Proverbs 25:17.
20   Philippians 4:13.

9

Verses from the Holy Scriptures to Overcome Loneliness

"I am the good shepherd; and I know My sheep, and am known by My own."[21]

"In that day sing to her, 'A vineyard of red wine! I, the LORD, keep it, I water it every moment; lest any hurt it, I keep it night and day."[22]

"I am with you always, even to the end of

---

21   John 10:14.
22   Isaiah 27:2–3.

the age."[23]

"'As one whom his mother comforts, so I will comfort you; and you shall be comforted in Jerusalem.' When you see this, your heart shall rejoice, and your bones shall flourish like grass; the hand of the LORD shall be known to His servants, and His indignation to His enemies."[24]

"If you love Me, keep My commandments. And I will pray the Father, and He will give you another Helper, that He may abide with you forever—the Spirit of truth, whom the world cannot receive, because it neither sees Him nor knows Him; but you know Him, for He dwells with you and will be in you. I will not leave you orphans; I will come to you."[25] (John 14:15–18.).

"The LORD is my shepherd; I shall not want. He makes me to lie down in green pastures; He leads me beside the still waters. He restores my soul; He leads me in the paths of righteousness for His name's sake.

---

23   Matthew 28:20.
24   Isaiah 66:13–14.
25   John 14:15–18.

Yea, though I walk through the valley of the shadow of death, I will fear no evil; for You are with me; Your rod and Your staff, they comfort me."[26]

"For God has not given us a spirit of fear, but of power and of love and of a sound mind."[27]

"The secret of the LORD is with those who fear Him, and He will show them His covenant. My eyes are ever toward the LORD, for He shall pluck my feet out of the net."[28]

---

26   Psalms 23:1–4.

27   2 Timothy 1:7.

28   Psalms 25:14–15.